To

Dad,

Thank you for being
who you are!

D1491604

'TO A VERY SPECIAL'® IS A REGISTERED TRADEMARK OF
EXLEY PUBLICATIONS LTD AND EXLEY PUBLICATIONS LLC.

OTHER GIFTBOOKS BY HELEN EXLEY:
The Best of Father Quotations
The Love Between Fathers and Daughters
The Love Between Fathers and Sons
The World's Greatest Dad Cartoons
To the World's Best Dad

Published simultaneously in 1998 by Exley Publications LLC in the USA,
and Exley Publications Ltd in Great Britain.

12 11 10 9 8 7 6 5 4 3 2

Copyright © Helen Exley 1998
The moral right of the author has been asserted.

ISBN 1-86187-031-0

Edited by Helen Exley.
Written by Pam Brown.
Illustrated by Judith O'Dwyer and Juliette Clarke.
Printed and bound in Hungary.

Exley Publications Ltd, 16 Chalk Hill, Watford, Herts WD1 4BN, UK.
Exley Publications LLC, 232 Madison Avenue, Suite 1206, NY 10016, USA.

THANK YOU
TO A VERY SPECIAL®

A HELEN EXLEY GIFTBOOK

Written by Pam Brown
Illustrations by Judith O'Dwyer
and Juliette Clarke
Edited by Helen Exley

EXLEY
NEW YORK • WATFORD, UK

THANK YOU FOR EVERYTHING

THANK YOU FOR SLIDING MY SPINACH ON TO YOUR PLATE WHEN GRANDMA'S BACK IS TURNED.

—

THANK YOU FOR BELIEVING THAT MEASLES HAS PRIORITY OVER A GOLF TOURNAMENT.

—

THANK YOU FOR MAKING MY CHILDHOOD SO RICH AND RARE. SO THAT I NEVER FOR ONCE SUSPECTED WE WERE OFFICIALLY POOR.

—

Thank you for always making time
to hear about our days, even when
you came home tired and longing
for a good meal.

–

Thank you for all the Best Bits
from your plate.

–

For you have been there for me,
always; loving me when I was near
impossible to love. Advising when I
could be persuaded to listen.
Helping me, even when I did not
deserve your help. Believing in me
when anyone else would have
walked away.

–

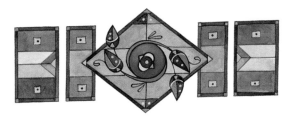

THANK YOU FOR BEING HUMAN

THANK YOU FOR NOT BEING THE PERFECT
FATHER.
NONE OF US COULD HAVE LIVED UP TO THAT.
WE LOVE YOU EXACTLY AS YOU ARE.

–

FORGIVE US, DAD, IF WE TEASE YOU – YOUR
SOCKS, YOUR TIES, YOUR DOLEFUL SWEATERS,
YOUR QUITE APPALLING HATS.
YOUR INABILITY TO HIT A NAIL WITHOUT INJURY.
YOUR ABSENT-MINDEDNESS.
YOUR GIFT OF PROCRASTINATION.
WE TEASE BECAUSE WE LOVE YOU.
IF YOU WERE AS INCOMPETENT AS WE PRETEND
YOU ARE – WE WOULD NOT SAY IT. WE DELIGHT
IN RECOGNIZING THAT YOU ARE COMPLETELY
HUMAN – OUR DEAR, KIND, LOVING, WISE AND
SILLY DAD.

–

THANK YOU FOR ALL THE FUNNY THINGS — THE SILLY JOKES, THE CLOWNING, THE OUTINGS THAT WENT WRONG. THE REPAIRS THAT FELL APART, THE CHERISHED SEEDLINGS THAT GREW TO WEEDS. THE TOM CAT THAT HAD KITTENS. NOT FUNNY TO THE OUTSIDE WORLD, PERHAPS. BUT TO US. OUR JOKES. THE MYTHS AND LEGENDS OF A FAMILY.

—

DEAR DAD — THANK YOU FOR CONFESSING WHEN YOU DIDN'T KNOW ANYTHING ABOUT THE CHARTISTS OR PHOTOSYNTHESIS OR GNEISS OR DIFFERENTIAL CALCULUS. BUT HELPING ME LOOK THEM UP.

—

PROTECTION

*Thank you for being the best Kisser-Better
in the business.*

—

*Far away or close to me you are a part of my life;
my hopes, my achievements, my courage in
adversity. I turn to you for encouragement and for
comfort – just as I did when I was very small.*

This is your chair.
And when life seems far too difficult
I roost in it
– settling into the hollows you have made.
– drawing comfort from your presence
– even when you are not there.

—

There are real dads. Who listen to reading practice
and tell stories and blow noses and sit up with
fevers and play beach tennis and cuddle away
miseries. And listen.
Like you.

—

I wish you'd never had to worry about me
– but I'm so thankful that you do.

—

... FOR VALUES AND WISDOM

Thank you for teaching me about friendship and kindness and concern – just by watching you.

—

Under all I do or think or say lies your example, your comradeship, your kindness, your patience.
You gave me the roots from which to grow.
You protected and strengthened me, taught me, shared my laughter and my sorrow.
Praised my victories, helped me find worth even in failure.
All that is worthwhile in me is founded on your wisdom, your love and your humanity.

—

You never guessed at answers to our questions, Dad. You said, "I don't know. Let's look it up." And so set us on the road to honest thinking.

–

Thank you for showing me how very small this planet is – and that all living things are our relations – and can be our friends.

–

Thank you for persuading me to be stubborn in truth, if I know for sure it's truth.

–

Thank you for showing me that if all is lost save love – nothing is lost.

–

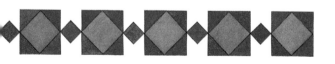

THANK YOU FOR SHARING MY CHILDHOOD DAYS

THANK YOU FOR ALL THE SWEET RITUALS OF CHILDHOOD. THE CLICK OF THE KEY IN THE DOOR. THE RUN DOWN THE PASSAGE INTO YOUR ARMS. THE SWING TO THE CEILING. THE SQUASH AS YOU KISSED MUM. THE SIP OF YOUR TEA. THE SHARING OF NEWS. THE CUDDLE-UP ON THE SOFA. THE SPLASHING OF BATH TIME. THE SHOULDER RIDE TO BED. THE SNUGGLE OF STORY TELLING. YOUR VOICE DOWNSTAIRS. THE SAFETY OF YOU BEING THERE.

—

THANK YOU FOR THE MEMORIES,
— THE JOYS YOU CRAFTED OUT OF LOVE,
— THE SMALL ADVENTURES YOU'VE DEVISED FOR ME,
— THE COMPANIONSHIP THAT WE SHARED.

—

THANK YOU FOR READING TO ME IN THE
EVENINGS WHEN I WAS VERY, VERY SMALL
AND SICK IN BED. BEING REALLY
COMFORTABLE STILL SUMMONS UP
MEMORIES OF A SHIELDED BEDSIDE LAMP,
THE CURTAIN DRAWN, RAIN ON THE
WINDOW, THE SMELL OF HYACINTHS AND
YOUR VOICE SOMEHOW TUNED TO THAT
OF POOH.

–

AND THOUGH I'VE GROWN AND FOUND
MY OWN WAY – MY MIND IS THAT OF A
LITTLE CHILD,
– AND I AM SAFE AND LOVED,
– AND HOME.

–

... FOR LETTING ME BE FREE

THANK YOU FOR NOT BEING SAD WHEN MY DREAMS TURNED OUT TO BE QUITE DIFFERENT TO THE ONES YOU HAD FOR ME. THANK YOU FOR HELPING ME TO BECOME WHAT I WANTED TO BE.

—

THANK YOU FOR NEVER WANTING TO BE ONE OF THE GANG — FOR NOT WANTING TO BE MY BEST PAL — FOR NOT WANTING TO SHARE IN ALL MY ACTIVITIES. FOR BEING WHAT I NEEDED YOU TO BE. MY DAD.

—

THANKS FOR OPENING ALL THOSE DOORS FOR ME — BUT NEVER SHOVING ME THROUGH THEM.

—

THANK YOU FOR ALWAYS BEING THERE WHEN
I NEEDED YOU – AND LETTING ME GO FREE
WHEN I NEEDED FREEDOM.

–

THANK YOU FOR LETTING ME DO THINGS
THAT TERRIFIED YOU.

At long last – there comes the turn of
the key in the lock and,
hey presto, he is back.
With a newspaper.
And perhaps a small surprise.
A kiss, a meal, a game, a story, a
splashing bath – and it's off to bed with
another kiss.
He is most wonderfully there at
weekends and on holidays, or if you are
very, very poorly, but on the whole he is
a beneficent but invisible presence.
Closely akin to a god.
Later, of course, he is a man to boast
about – and at rare intervals he may
take you to The Office, Or The Shop,
or The Laboratory.
And show you off to people. A mutual
admiration society of two….
But now comes the time when you
suddenly perceive that he is not very
good at spelling,

*and inclined to get his history dates
wrong. And doesn't play tennis like
Chris's dad. And is liable to shout, and
to nag about your room....
He makes terrible mistakes. His politics
are hopeless. He is out of touch with the
young. He is dull. He is a bore. And he
has peculiar habits....
But, just in time, a miracle occurs, and
almost overnight you begin to see that
you too are human, and fallible, and
that you and he have a lot in common.
That he knows a thing or two,
... and you are friends for life.*

—

*Dearest Dad – we are contemporaries,
you and I.
Always have been.
Always will be.*

—

YOU GAVE ME THE STRENGTH

WHATEVER I ACHIEVE – YOU GAVE ME
THE COURAGE TO BEGIN.

–

TIME AND DISTANCE CANNOT SEPARATE US. YOU
ARE THE CERTAINTY THAT MAKES ALL
UNCERTAINTY BEARABLE. YOU ARE THE ONE I
TRUST WHEN ALL ELSE FAILS. YOU HAVE GIVEN
ME THE STRENGTH AND CONFIDENCE TO STAND
ALONE – BUT I KNOW THAT YOU ARE THERE,
QUIET AND KIND, READY TO HELP ME
IF I FAIL OR FALTER.

–

Here is your hand – dear and familiar from
my earliest days.
I learned it, inch by inch, in childhood.
The little golden hairs on the back
of your fingers.
The shape of each nail.
The swirl of each knuckle.
The veins beneath the skin.
The little scar,
The marks of work and winter.
The feel, the scent of it.
How strong, how safe, it seemed.
And as I hold it now – I seem to feel my life
held in its safe keeping.

–

ALWAYS, ALWAYS THERE

THIS IS THE DAY WE CELEBRATE
ANOTHER YEAR OF HAVING THE BEST DAD IN THE
WORLD. THE DAY WE LOOK BACK AND REMEMBER
THE WAYS YOU'VE MADE IT SPECIAL.
THE SURPRISES AND DELIGHTS YOU'VE GIVEN US
— AND THE QUIET, CONSTANT THINGS THAT
HAVE MEANT SO MUCH TO
ALL YOUR FAMILY.
AND WE SAY THANK YOU.

—

Thank you for being there in the background – sure and certain – always and always.

–

Thank you for holding me steady till I found my feet, for guiding me until I could find the way, for letting me walk on, out of sight.
For being there with unchanging love whether I came home in victory or in failure.

–

You are the rock on which I've built my life – never failing in your love, your support, your wisdom and your laughter.

–

You will never grow old.
In my memory we still sprawl in the sun
under the apple boughs,
still splash along the water's edge,
still watch the bonfire flare,
the sparks eddying in the November sky.
We still hold hands to race across the park
and drowse together by the fire
and lose ourselves in stories
of the long ago.
Time makes its changes
– but cannot hurt the people that we were
and are forever.

—

No one can take our jokes, our happy
silliness, our games, our small adventures,
away from us.

—

I hear your whistle
– and I am a child again
– waiting for the sound of your key in
the lock
– your kiss, your hug
– the sharing of our day.

—

*T*hank you for quiet times
– just you and me.

–

*T*hank you for sharing sleepy days in
summer meadows, kicking up showers of
red-gold leaves, walks on winter beaches,
kites on springtime uplands. Thank you
for catching the passing moment for me –
and making it last forever
in my mind.

–

*C*hildren are inclined to take
their dad for granted.
But today I want to give you
all the thank yous,
– for all the things we did together when
I was very small – for the laughter and the
patience and the quiet comfort.
Thank you Dad!

–

*THANK YOU FOR
FORGIVING – FOR
BELIEVING IN ME*

*D*earest Dad – thank you for letting me
realize it's OK to fail – to see that every
failure teaches something – and sets one
free to begin again.

–

*T*hank you for never giving up hope –
even when I was at my very, very worst.

–

*T*hank you for not killing us when we
stepped on the setting concrete, when we
watered the begonias from the weed-killer
can, when we cut wire with the secateurs.
I know it went through your mind.
But you didn't.

–

*T*hank you for giving me second chances.
And third chances.
And fourth chances....

–

You have the ability to comfort,
to encourage and to praise.
I fail an examination – "I wouldn't worry.
You learn by your mistakes.
You'll do well next time."
I am deserted by my best friend – "Well,
it's obvious. He wasn't worth it.
I never liked him.
Now you're free to meet far nicer people."
I lose my job – "I'll never know how you
stuck it so long. Waste of your time. No
future in it. At any rate, it was experience
– be useful in the next job – whatever
you decide to do."
The doctor has slightly alarming news –
"Ah! Now we are getting somewhere.
You know where you are.
Far better than to be left in limbo.
Now we can do something about it."
I may not have believed it all. Hearts and
egos are not so easily healed. But it gave
me hope. It gave me courage.
For I knew I was loved.

–

. . . Y O U   H A V E
S U R R O U N D E D   M E
W I T H   L O V E

Even the word "Dad"
warms my heart
— for you have wrapped me
in your love
and given me a lasting gift.
I cannot succumb to any cold,
to any darkness
while I remember you.

—

Time passes, but your love never
falters, never fades. You are as
dear, as necessary to my life,
as when I ran into your arms and
soared onto your shoulders — happy
and secure.

—